Anger
Management

Anger Management

A Simple Guide To Managing Life's Expectations

Mark Stricklin

ANGER MANAGEMENT
A SIMPLE GUIDE TO MANAGING LIFE'S EXPECTATIONS

The information, ideas, and suggestions in this book are not intended as a substitute for professional advice. Before following any suggestions contained in this book, you should consult your personal physician or mental health professional. Neither the author nor the publisher shall be liable or responsible for any loss or damage allegedly arising as a consequence of your use or application of any information or suggestions in this book.

iUniverse books may be ordered through booksellers or by contacting:

iUniverse
1663 Liberty Drive
Bloomington, IN 47403
www.iuniverse.com
1-800-Authors (1-800-288-4677)

Because of the dynamic nature of the Internet, any web addresses or links contained in this book may have changed since publication and may no longer be valid. The views expressed in this work are solely those of the author and do not necessarily reflect the views of the publisher, and the publisher hereby disclaims any responsibility for them.

Any people depicted in stock imagery provided by Thinkstock are models, and such images are being used for illustrative purposes only. Certain stock imagery © Thinkstock.

ISBN: 978-1-4917-9522-4 (sc)
ISBN: 978-1-4917-9521-7 (hc)
ISBN: 978-1-4917-9540-8 (e)

Library of Congress Control Number: 2016909575

Print information available on the last page.

iUniverse rev. date: 08/04/2016

ROAD RAGE

by: Mark Stricklin

illustrated by: Mike Schwartz

EXPECTATIONS

by: Mark Stricklin

illustrated by: Mike Schwartz

PET PEVE'S

by: Mark Stricklin
illustrated by: Mike Schwartz

Contents

Foreword

From Township Supervisor Patricia Jones,
Waukegan Township, Illinois

There's an old saying that if you want something done right, do it yourself. However, if you want something done a very particular way, it may be best for you to work with people who share your standards of quality. Well, I have the distinct opportunity to introduce and acknowledge my good friend and brother from another mother, Mark Stricklin—someone who is qualified to do it right, regardless of the task or assignment.

Mark and I met several years ago when he showed up at the Waukegan Township office to serve as a volunteer assistant for our youth program. Since that time, Mark has volunteered his time and dedicated his talent and skills to renovate an age-old fire station and convert it into a homeless facility. The Eddie Washington Center received an award from the governor of Illinois for its volunteer-led achievements, in large part because of Mark Stricklin. A few years later, the township purchased a facility dedicated to the enhancement, safety, and empowerment of women and their children. This was another old but charmed house in the Waukegan community. Mark was, in large part, the go-to person during the renovation of this facility, which has now been in existence for twenty years.

And it gets even better. Mark volunteered to facilitate anger management courses for our residents and other members of the community, usually people referred to him by the Nineteenth Judicial Circuit Court. Mark created a curriculum and offers courses free of charge, and he has done so for more than fifteen years.

So if you want something done right ... call Mark Stricklin! He's a God-fearing family man and the essence of a public servant.

Acknowledgments

Writing a book is, of course, a community project. My wife, Susan, and wonderful children, Tanya and Deidra (and Deidra's husband, Greg), provided wonderful support throughout the writing of this book and the many nights I was away teaching classes or seminars.

I also want to acknowledge the many years of support that I have received from Supervisor Patricia Jones and the Eddie Washington Center, which gave me the opportunity to share my passion. Supervisor Jones has been my inspiration and my best source of encouragement.

Also, I want to say that any of the suggestions or advice in this book should be considered personal insights and wisdom gained from years of teaching, not professional psychological or medical advice. My advice comes from close to twenty years of teaching anger management classes, leading seminars, and working one-on-one with people struggling with anger issues. This has been a two-way street; I have learned a lot from many of those who attended my classes. I am deeply indebted to them for helping me on my own journey.

Introduction

Hi, my name is Mark, and I am a bonehead. I am the chief bonehead of BoneHeads Anonymous (I wanted to call it Anger Anonymous, but AA was already taken). I have written this book because, as a bonehead, I do stupid things all the time, and then I watch others doing stupid things. And that makes me mad. I spend a lot of time being angry at others and myself. For example, while working on this book, I bought an expensive pair of sunglasses. I justified the purchase because I could use them so many places. Oh, they were so nice—unbreakable, with special Polaroid lenses. I even did some research on the Internet; they received great reviews. But I knew I shouldn't buy them. Although they may have been unbreakable, they were not bonehead-proof. I lose my sunglasses all the time. I can't keep them for any length of time. There is no warranty for being a bonehead.

But, I said to myself, *I won't lose them. No, not these sunglasses—they are too expensive. I'll take real good care of them.* Three days later, I lost them. What a bonehead! I was so mad at myself. I knew better.

This book is about what makes us angry, how to deal with and manage our anger, and how to deal with angry people. Although I have a degree in psychology, I learned most of these lessons during my interactions with the people I teach in my weekly classes at a transitional shelter. I have met people from all walks of life there; they bring a wealth of knowledge and experiences to the classes. Through those classes, I've learned, relearned, changed, and reevaluated how I embrace anger and anger management. Then I share that information with others in seminars, workshops, and personal mentoring sessions, and now I'm sharing it in this book. I truly believe the advice on the following pages will help anyone gain a simple understanding of what causes anger and practical ways to manage it.

This book deals with anger management, not anger elimination.

Chapter 1

How to Live a Life Free of Anger

If you picked up this book because you want to know how to get rid of anger, you picked up the wrong book. This book is about anger management—recognizing the source of your anger and then evaluating your responses to it. But as a side note to the main thrust of this book, I can tell you how to be anger-free. You only need to read these few short pages.

There are three ways to live a life free from anger. The first is to be in a coma. The second is to stop caring about anything.

Seriously! If you stop caring, you will not get angry. Haven't you ever met two people who've experienced the same situation, but one is upset and angry and the other is not? When you ask the second person why, he will tell you that he doesn't care. It doesn't bother him. No skin off his back. He is not emotionally invested in the situation; therefore he is not mad. The angry person cares, while the non-angry person does not.

You may know someone who has experienced this, or you may have experienced it yourself—not caring about something. It is called apathy (or as some people would say, "Whatever!"). Apathy is not caring. *Que sera, sera.*

Whatever will be, will be. Apathy is absence of emotion. Stop caring, and you'll stop being angry. But the fact that we are westerners—driven to achieve, to consume, and to gain status—sets the stage for countless unmet expectations. When we care about stuff, we have the potential for being disappointed and feeling angry.

We don't always start out being apathetic, with the intention of not caring. Instead we can move in that direction over time. After many disappointments, we develop an unintentional self-defense mechanism that saves our soul, our emotional reservoir. We can make the decision to stop caring because it hurts too much. Sometimes it is a gradual slide into apathy, and other times it is a spontaneous decision not to care.

For example, have you ever been so mad at someone (or someone has been so mad at you) that you arrive at the place where you make the decision to stop caring? You may even have told that person, "I don't care what you do or where you go. Stay out of my life." Or perhaps you stopped getting involved in or you cut off relationships because you don't care anymore. This could be a former boyfriend/girlfriend or husband/wife, or any other person who was involved in your life. It could even be a job, hobby, or organization that you walked away from. You became so angry that you had to quit being emotionally invested. You stopped caring.

If you have an emotional investment in someone, than there is a risk that he or she can hurt you and make you angry. We end up being angry because things didn't work out. Life is all about having expectations and trying to fulfill them.

Often we'll reflect back on our lives and whether or not they have met our expectations. If they have, then we are generally happy; if they haven't, then we might be bitter and angry. What kind of person do you want to be—a bitter person or a better person? A better person is one who has gone through life understanding and accepting that it will not meet all their expectations. A bitter person is one who decides that life isn't fair and has cheated him out of opportunities. A bitter person believes that life is hard and has robbed him of some or most of his expectations. A better person believes that life is hard but good, and things turned out all right. Life met most of his expectations.

You can feel anger about society in general, an organization, or your workplace, or any activity in which you participate. Then you can get tired of being angry, make a conscious decision to stop caring about the world around you, and drop out emotionally and/or physically. That is apathy in its full glory. Moving to a log cabin in the woods and living off the land doesn't sound so bad sometimes, because it removes the many expectations you have regarding others in your life. Living in a log cabin would mean that you would only have to deal with yourself and Mother Nature.

A funny story that happened to me a few years ago, when I took my family to Disney World in Florida, illustrates what apathy is all about. I was waiting in line with my granddaughter, Gabrielle (who, by the way, gave me permission to tell this story). Since the lines were consistently long, I would pass the time by making small talk with people in line around me.

Finally Gabrielle asked me, "How come you are always talking to people?"

I responded, "To pass the time. I find it interesting to learn where people come from and what they do."

She gave me that look—you know, the look teenagers give when they feel their parents are embarrassing them.

Since I was embarrassing her, I said, "Okay, then, let's you and I talk." I asked her the following questions (keeping in mind that she was very young, and slightly embarrassed that her grandpa was disturbing the peace):

"Do you want to talk about politics?"

"No" was her response.

"Do you want to talk about religion?"

"No" was her response.

"Do you want to talk about current events?"

"No" was her response.

I followed with a couple more questions, and she gave the same response. I then asked her why she didn't want to talk. She said that she didn't care. I then proceeded to ask her if she knew what apathy meant. She said no, and that she didn't care.

Many people around us in line started to giggle, as they couldn't help listening in on our conversation. She actually knew the meaning of the word *apathy*, but she didn't know that she knew. Thank you, Gabrielle, for letting me share that.

This apathy (not caring) is a basic human defensive response. When we stop caring for someone or when we withdraw from society, we may be helping preserve ourselves and our sanity. We can make a conscious decision to stop caring, and the end result or side effect is the elimination of our anger. This apathy helps us retain our sense of self-worth and our emotional energy, which is being depleted by the person or situation that is the focus of our anger.

Now if you want to be anger-free, take this apathy and apply it to every area of your life. If you do not care about anything, you will never be angry. If you don't care about the people around you, about where you live or society or politics or religion and so forth—the list can go on and on—then you will not have to deal with anger. It is when you care that you place yourself in a position to feel the emotion of anger. Caring carries with it expectations that may not be met. If you care, then you will have expectations.

The third way of living a life without anger is to modify or change your expectations so that in every aspect of your life, life meets your expectations.

**Any time we get angry, it is because
we have an unmet expectation.**

The bottom line is that you would be perfectly happy if everything happened just the way you want it. Living life your way, as well as everyone else in the world living life your way, would remove any reasons for being angry.

Instead of trying to have every aspect of your life live up to your standards and expectations, which is nearly impossible, you can modify your expectations.

**You must acknowledge that in life, not
all your expectations will be met—and
decide that you are okay with that.**

This way, although you might have expectations, you will not expect them all to be met. Then the anger in your life will be very manageable; you will be able to live with anger and know and accept that it is okay to be angry. Or perhaps your anger will be eliminated altogether.

Although I have told you how to live anger-free, you might suspect from the tone of my writing that I do not think it is healthy to live life without the emotion of anger. Who really wants to live anger-free? To do so, you would have to live a life that is basically flat-lined: no pulse, no ups or downs. You really wouldn't be living life to the fullest in any sense of the word. Not caring about anything would make life boring. How can you experience deep and lasting peace and joy if you do not have something to compare them to?

Now for the reality check: we know that it is basically impossible for all of life to live up to our expectations. So the rest of this book explores what we can learn about our expectations and how to manage them. The practical result can lead us to embrace anger as simply one of the emotions that humans are capable of, and to live life more fully. Anger is an emotion that we need to understand and embrace. It is neither right nor wrong; it is something we experience. The "right or wrong" part of anger has to do with how we deal with it. How we respond to the emotion of anger is what we, and those around us, judge as good or bad.

So if this strategy sounds good to you, the rest of this book is for you. Anger management is all about managing your expectations.

Chapter 2

The Law of Anger

Unmet Expectations = Anger

"Every time we get angry—without exception—it's when we have an unmet expectation. And twenty bucks goes to anyone who can prove me wrong." This is my opening statement in my anger management workshops. I place a twenty-dollar bill on the board behind me or flash a picture of one on a screen, and then I challenge anyone in the room to give me a personal example of a time they felt angry and did not have some unmet expectation. Over decades and hundreds of classes and seminars, I have never lost my money (although I have given away money for some creative and funny answers). Truth be told, no one ever wins the twenty bucks—no one! And the amazing thing is that no one has ever gotten angry about not winning the money. Why? Maybe because they knew it was a trick question and so they really did not expect to win it.

What makes us angry? There are only two reasons, apart from a chemical imbalance or similar clinical diagnosis, or immaturity (not having reached the age of reason). First, we have an expectation of how something should happen. Second, we have an expectation of how something should not happen. So any time we use the words *should* or *should not*, we have an expectation. Within that expectation lies the potential to feel anger when the expectation is not met.

Anger management is all about managing our expectations, knowing our options, and choosing the right response for every situation. The lessons in this book are simple and not my own, and the truth is that while everything I've shared within these pages deals directly with anger, it also can be applied to any other emotion. Anger management is all about emotion management. Joy, happiness, depression, grief, and so forth are emotions that can lead to poor judgment and bad behavior. Really, we should call this subject "emotion management," but "anger management" is the more popular and politically correct term, so we'll stick with that.

Most people who attend anger management classes are there because they've been forced to come by the court system, their parole officers, or their employers. Very few of them choose to attend on their own. Most people will admit that they get angry but do not feel that they have a problem. I hear this all the time. People will say, "I don't have a problem," but then they will add something like, "My brother-in-law (husband, wife, brother) really needs your class. *That's* who should be here. Not me." It is always somebody else who has the problem. I find it funny that I rarely meet people who are honest with themselves and will admit that they have a problem dealing with anger.

My desire with this book, which is a product of my anger management classes and seminars, is to share with you ways to manage anger and expectations. The theory is simple, but the practical application takes energy and commitment to change.

When we feel angry, we usually feel justified in our emotion; otherwise we wouldn't be angry. Those around us, therefore, are just reaping the consequences of our righteous anger. But the truth is that all of us, or at least 99 percent of us, experience anger. The 1 percent who never get angry are the people I described in the introduction—people who are in an emotional coma, who don't care and don't have any expectations. But the rest of us experience situations in everyday life where our expectations are not met, and that makes us feel angry and upset. This is our reality.

Anger has many names or synonyms in our culture. We might say we're upset, irritated, mad, or enraged. We might stew, go postal, blow up, or have a catfight—there are a few dozen other names too. In our culture, these names represent an attempt to quantify and qualify the intensity of a person's anger. But that level is extremely personal and subjective; it cannot be measured concretely. Maybe someday scientists will be able to measure people's brain waves and assign a number to their anger according to its level of intensity. But as of now, the intensity of someone's anger is extremely personal and hard to measure.

Your level of anger may or may not be the same as mine, but we might use the same words to describe it. There is no way of measuring the level of intensity accurately. We can assess that a person is angry, but can we really know what goes on inside a person's head?

Learning to deal with and accept anger, as important as this skill is, is not something children are taught in school or at home. The curriculum when I was growing up was based on moral guidelines. It taught kids that they shouldn't be angry, instead of teaching them how to accept their anger and then manage their expectations and responses. Didn't we hear over and over as children that we shouldn't be angry?

**But it is okay to be angry,
and we need to learn to manage that emotion.**

There is nothing moral or immoral about the emotion of anger, nothing good or bad. How we respond to anger is where the question of morality comes in, and where we're judged by those around us and society as a whole.

We learn our anger management response by seeing how others display their anger in person or in the media, such as on TV. Generally, the entertainment media teach us that when we get angry, we should get even—that is, get revenge or payback. This seems to be the basic plot of most movies that center around anger: the good guy gets angry and then gets even.

Yet we tell children that they shouldn't be angry, or that they simply have to "deal with it." What an injustice to our children! What a mistake! We should teach our children that it is okay to be angry and then teach them that life doesn't always live up to our expectations. Then we should teach them appropriate options for dealing with and expressing their anger.

If my younger sister takes my toy without my permission and breaks it, I should be allowed to feel angry. But then I should be instructed how to appropriately display that anger toward my sister. I should be taught to consider my expectations in that situation and to modify them to reflect reality—in this case, the fact that my sister is too young and immature to understand what she did wrong. Maybe at this point in time, I have unrealistic expectations considering her level of development.

I shouldn't be told to suck it up, because eventually there will come a time when I can't suck it up anymore, and then my behavior may be disproportionate to the offense committed, or even way over the top. We need to teach children and adults to manage their expectations.

Wouldn't it be great to teach children at an early age that it is okay to feel the emotion of anger, or emotions in general, and then teach them productive ways to manage those feelings? Maybe we can start today, with you. Since I am the anger management expert, I give you permission to be angry, starting today. There—I said it! You can be angry. Now, don't go out and do something stupid because I gave you permission to be angry; read the rest of the book. Being angry is not the problem, but how you deal with anger is the problem.

I have had numerous discussions with judges, lawyers, and police officers, and not one of them thinks we should try to eliminate the emotion of anger. We just need to learn when to express it and when to hold it back—sort of like Kenny Rogers sings in "The Gambler." We need to know when to hold 'em and when to fold 'em.

Our expectations are many, vast, and complicated. They are like an onion—made up of many layers. We can peel one layer off, thinking that we understand it, only to find that there is another deeper and more complex layer of expectations underneath. The human brain is amazing and intricate; there are no quick, easy steps to managing our anger. There are no standardized formulas, no magic potions that will manage our anger for us. As a matter of fact, I believe we should not be trying to eliminate our anger at all, but instead trying to recognize the unmet expectation that caused our anger, identify our options, and choose the best response to that unmet expectation.

People do not go to anger elimination class; they go to anger management class. Nobody really thinks we should be anger-free. Yet I believe there is a simple truth to this difficult subject—a truth that will help those desiring to better understand themselves and any culture in the world regarding the issue of anger.

We don't need elaborate rules or formulas to memorize or follow; we need a simple, commonsense way to deal with unmet expectations. We should begin by asking ourselves these questions when we are angry:

What are my expectations right now?
What are my choices for responding?
What are the consequences of each choice?

Often when I am in a mentoring situation, I will ask the person who is angry, "What advice would you give someone else in the same situation?" (I have found quite regularly that people give great advice to others but fall short in taking their own advice). We can be our best counselors if we really listen to ourselves and don't continually make up reasons why we are exceptions to the rule. You know what I mean: everyone should listen to our advice, but our own situation is different.

The beginning of managing your anger, therefore, is looking at your expectations. That sounds simple, but it can be difficult when the rubber meets the road. This is a lifelong journey of perfecting the thought process of understanding why we become angry and what our choices are when we are angry. Will this choice, this course of action, benefit me and/or those around me? Will it inflame the situation? Will it damage or help my relationship?

In the following chapters, we will explore such choices. We will take a look at our reasoning and how it affects our emotions. As the old proverb goes, "As a man thinks, so is he."

I really would like to commend you for taking the effort to read this book, and I hope it can help you experience the fullness of living life in its emotional completeness, including feeling, acknowledging, and expressing anger appropriately. It's okay to be angry. Being angry is not the problem. But what we do with that feeling determines if our response is good or bad, healthy or unhealthy.

Chapter 3

Expectations Defined Further

An expectation is a funny thing. It is different from a hope. A hope is a wish that something will happen. An expectation is a belief that something will happen. If I play the lottery, I hope to win, and I want to win, but because of the odds, I do not really expect to win. Nevertheless, I'll spend time before the drawing thinking about what I would do with the money if I were to win. I know that I am paying for that fantasy.

As I mentioned before, two people can experience the same challenging situation and react in opposite ways: one can be angry while the other is completely free of anger. Why? Because the angry person expected something to happen (or not to happen), and the other person didn't care what happened or was okay with what happened. Just ask someone who is not angry despite having experienced a negative situation: he will surely answer that he simply didn't care or that he'd expected that to happen.

Caring about something has expectations attached to it. There are many unmet expectations that can lead to being disappointed, frustrated, upset, mad, and so forth. (note: that all these words, and many similar words, reflect different forms of anger.) Caring puts us in a place of expectation, which potentially sets us up to be angry. If our expectations are met, we are happy or satisfied; if they are not, we experience some form of anger. If I care about my motorcycle, then I will be angry when a child on a bike rides by my motorcycle and scratches it. If I care about my house, I will clean it and take care of it, and I will be upset when others do not care and mess it up. When we care about something or someone, we lay the foundation for potential anger down the road.

Occasionally, I run across people who claim that they never get angry. At first I didn't believe it when people told me that. But after some discussion, several poignant questions, and even intentional provocation, I determined that these people seemed to be telling the truth (although I was not with them 24/7, so I couldn't verify their statements). People like this seem to be content with themselves and others. They are content with the direction of their lives, accept what comes with living day to day, and truly are not concerned about what others think. Sometimes they do not even care what happens to them. They tell me that they do not have any expectations about life. They take what comes and do not get angry.

I understand not being overly concerned with what others think and being able to stand alone. I can handle that—although I'm certainly not there. But I really struggle to believe individuals who say they are never angry with themselves. I think that learning not to be angry at yourself is possibly the hardest lesson in life. I can't imagine being completely satisfied with every decision or action that I make. People tell me that they get angrier at themselves than they do at others.

Some people believe that they have met all their expectations concerning themselves. They take life as it comes, with no expectations. I have come to call this "the Doris Day Syndrome"—you know, "Que sera, sera ...

whatever will be, will be!" It doesn't matter what happens, these people are okay with it. They are content or at peace with who they are. Maybe they have reached a place of enlightenment or self-actualization, where they are at perfect peace with themselves. I can't relate to that right now in my life; maybe, they should be the ones teaching the anger management seminars!

Today, I still struggle with anger and unmet expectations, and I've drawn this conclusion: if you don't want to be angry, then don't care about anything and don't have any expectations (a philosophy I've already shared). But I want to care; therefore I know I take the emotional risk of being angry every day.

I don't know about you, but I find myself getting angry with myself for many of the boneheaded things, especially all the dumb things, I say and do. I get angry with myself for making the wrong decisions, I get angry with myself for all the opportunities I've missed, and—to put it in simple terms—I get angry with myself because I am not where I should be in life, spiritually, emotionally, or financially. The list could go on and on.

I also have a lot of expectations about life in general. Not a day goes by that I do not experience some unmet expectation. I suspect that the same is true for you too.

But the good news is that I really believe we can experience life to the fullest. Because we have feelings and emotions, we need to embrace them, and that includes anger. Doing so, allows us to be fully present and live in the moment. I would rather experience the ups and downs of life than live with a flat affect—no emotions, no feelings, the "whatever" attitude. (By the way, doesn't it bother you when someone constantly says "whatever"? That's a pet peeve of mine: "Whatever!")

Simply put, we were born with emotions, and each emotion runs the gamut of intensity and duration. Let us learn to embrace our emotions and passions while accepting and affirming those of others. Let us be role models to others so they too can live a life fulfilled.

In summary, we have learned the following lessons so far:

- This book is not about how to eliminate anger, but how to handle anger when we experience it.
- Unmet expectations make us mad.
- Caring is a form of expectation.
- Our "shoulds" and "should nots" are expectations.

Chapter 4

Modifying Our Expectations

This Is Anger Management

The safest and fastest way to lower the intensity of or eliminate our anger is to change or modify our expectations. We can change our expectations by including exceptions to the rules represented by our "shoulds" and "should nots." The caveat to modifying our expectations is that we really have to believe in the change. If, deep down, we still hang on to the former expectation in its original form, we have accomplished nothing.

For example, some people expect others to return phone calls or text messages when asked to do so. To these people, this is a reasonable expectation, and they get angry when someone consistently chooses not to call them back or return messages without a justifiable excuse. They get upset at the other person's lack of social skills or conscious disrespect, which conveys the message "I'm more important than you, and my time is more important than you." Someone who's too busy to return a call or message demonstrates general rudeness and a better-than-thou attitude, and the fact that the person can so easily dismiss phone calls and not return them will make some people mad.

Now, perhaps those people could modify their original expectation to something like this: while they still might have an expectation that people should return their phone calls, they can also acknowledge that there are many circumstances that might prevent people from doing so, and therefore not everyone will return phone calls or text messages. This modification will temper their anger response. They may still get upset, but modifying their expectation will lower the intensity of their anger and keep them from going berserk.

Sometimes it helps us to postpone getting upset or angry till a later time—in this case, until it's clear why the person didn't get back to us or didn't realize that our phone call was important. This will lower our level of anger. By postponing our anger, we may realize that there are many legitimate reasons why the person didn't call back. Maybe the person forgot or didn't get the message. Maybe the miscommunication was our fault. And truth be told, sometimes we forget to call people back too. So a little grace can go a long way. Therefore, before we get bent out of shape over someone else's poor social skills or perceived lack of respect, we should be patient and wait for all the information. In postponing our justifiable right to get angry, we may find, in the long run, that the problem just wasn't important enough to get upset about in the first place.

Modifying our expectations to include reasonable exceptions to our rules will temper our anger (pun intended).

If we make these constant, ever-changing modifications to our expectations, we will find ourselves less angry.

The stronger the expectation, the more intense the level of anger.

I will get much angrier with someone who's close to me than with someone off the street. That's because I have higher expectations for the people I care about and who care about me. Think about this for a second. Who can make you the angriest? Probably the person closest to you: your wife or husband, your sister or brother, your mother or father, your neighbor, and so on and so forth. Our expectations are stronger for those closest to us.

Here's another question we should consider to help us manage our expectations: do we live up to the expectations that we impose on others? The truthful answer is probably not. And if we don't live up to the expectations that we impose on others, then our justification for anger falls short. Of course, we don't like that answer, because we can justify our own shortcomings a lot more easily that we can justify the shortcomings of others.

We can easily justify failing to meet others' expectations. We believe that our excuses—our exceptions to our rules—are valid, and that others should understand why we don't return all their phone calls, messages, e-mails, and so forth. If they knew the reason, they would understand and extend grace, mercy, and forgiveness to us. Here is a novel idea: why can't we extend the same grace, mercy, and forgiveness in advance to others, even before we have all the information? Try it and you may find that you are happier and more at peace.

Modifying your expectations sometimes means being willing to postpone judgment until a future time. There are two reasons why you may want to postpone your anger. One is that the present situation doesn't warrant or allow any opportunity to express your feelings. Perhaps something challenging happens while you're at work, and dealing with the issue while you're angry could result in a bad job performance or even losing your job. Think about the consequences if you were to express your anger in that situation. Thinking about it later would allow you to get a better perspective of how important the offense was and your options for dealing with it. Postponing your anger, and your response to that anger, allows you time to gather more information so that later you can reevaluate and process that information.

The second reason it's good to postpone your angry thoughts and responses is that it gives your mind and body a rest. Rest is important; it renews us mentally and physically so that we can gain better clarity of the situation and address the problem. We all need rest. Postponing or displacing your angry thoughts provides that emotional rest. Leaving a situation for a while and then coming back to it often gives you a fresh perspective. That could mean leaving the room to avoid saying something regrettable, or it could mean going to the gym to work out or going outside to take a bike ride.

Okay, now you are saying to yourself, *I'm willing to postpone my anger temporarily, but I can't stop thinking about it.* You're right; it is difficult to stop feeling hurt and angry. May I suggest that you replace or displace your thoughts for a short time? It is almost impossible to stop thinking about how you feel, but you can focus on new thoughts that produce different feelings.

This is where having a conversation with yourself is important. For example, you may want to think about whether the offense is worth losing your job or damaging your relationship. Are you making a mountain out of a molehill? Be open to the possibility that you don't have all the facts—and that if you did, you might be far less angry, or possibly not angry at all.

Another technique is taking a vacation in your mind, going to a happy place. Try visualizing your happy place. For example, think about your last vacation in the Bahamas, your favorite fishing hole, or some activity that you love. The key here is to visualize your happy place in as much detail as possible. Think of its colors, sounds, and textures—the more details the better. A word of warning: don't do this while driving or operating heavy machinery.

Modifying your expectations can help reduce the occurrence and intensity of anger. Postponing your anger until a later time may save your job or your relationship. And taking a vacation in your mind can be very productive, as it allows your mind and body to rest and then come back stronger to deal with the situation.

Chapter 5

Stress

Stress Equals Pressure
Change the Way You Think, Change the Way You Feel

Cogito ergo sum is Latin for "I think, therefore I am." René Descartes said that in 1637. Our thoughts affect the way we feel. As I've discussed before, when we think that our expectations are not being met, we feel angry. Our thoughts, feelings, and behavior can be thought of as a straight line most of the time, but not always. Human emotions and behavior are very complicated and not easily measured or repeated in experiments. In this chapter, I want to consider the idea that our feelings are directly caused by our thoughts, and sometimes having those different feelings makes us angry, because we don't like feeling that way. So on top of our other emotions is another layer of anger.

For example, if we are feeling stress, we are sensing some form of pressure. This pressure can be a real physical threat from our present situation, or just a perceived threat. Either way it is real to us.

What we percieve to be true is true to us.

Structural engineers can measure the stress or pressure that heavy traffic puts on bridges and roads, but we cannot measure stress or pressure on human beings because it is subjective and located in the mind. That's difficult to gauge in a concrete or repeatable way. Two people can experience the exact same event at the exact same time and have different levels of stress as a result. One person may not feel any stress at all, while the other is completely stressed out.

Why?

Because what we think affects the way we feel.

In psychology, this school of thought is called cognitive behaviorism. What we think affects the way we feel, and then our feelings affect the way we behave. As defined by the National Alliance of Mental Illness, cognitive behaviorism explores how our thoughts influence our behavior.

This school of thought is quite different than the one taught in the early days of pyschology, which studied the effects of outside physical stimulae, responses, punishments, and reinforcements on behavior. This early school of thought evolved into the stimulus and response theory and classical conditioning. It was easier to study in some senses, because scientists could see the physical stimulus and observe the physical response and develop ways to measure what they saw. I'm sure you have heard of the experiments of Ivan Pavlov, who rang a bell before feeding his dogs. Eventually the dogs would salivate at the sound of the bell alone, because they associated it with food.

Cognitive behavorism is different. We cannot see our thoughts; we only see the outcome of them, which is the observable behavior. Cognitive behaviorism is the study of the connection between our thoughts, our feelings, and our behavior.

Both the old and new ways of approaching and studying behavior work, but anger management concentrates on our thought life and how that influences our feelings and behavior.

Stress is usually thought of as negative, but it can also be positive. Some people thrive on stress; the pressure helps motivate them to accomplish tasks. Others are crippled by it.

If you feel stress and believe you can't take it anymore, then that is true to you. It can be difficult to change that way of thinking. But if you believe stress can sometimes be good, then your feelings and behavior under pressure will be different. How you feel about the stress or pressures in your life directly relates to how much stress you feel you can handle. The more pressure there is in your life, the greater your sense of stress. The longer the list of pressure-filled areas in your life, the more stress you will perceive and feel.

My doctor has stopped asking me if I have any stress in my life, because I keep telling him that everybody has stress and that I'm okay with it—the good, the bad, and the ugly. Stress is just part of life, no matter who you are or where you are in life. We all can feel stress regarding money, time constraints, relationships, jobs ... the list is endless. But as the saying goes, "What doesn't kill you only makes you stronger." I'm okay with stress and accept it as part of living.

To live a stress-free life, we need to stop percieving experiences or events as pressures. We need to recognize that it's all good. Stress is neither good or bad; it all depends on how we react to it. Choose to go with the flow. Pressure is necessary in life, and that is okay.

Chapter 6

Depression

Depression Is a Sense of Loss—Real or Perceived

Sometimes depression is confused with anger. When we feel the negative emotion of depression, it can feel similar to the negative emotion of anger. But they are different. Depression is a sense of loss. For example, if you experience the loss of a loved one, a job, or an opportunity, you may feel depressed, not angry. Anger often accompanies depression, however, because we are upset about being depressed. We need to give ourselves permission to feel emotions, including depression. Depression is a feeling we all experience at one time or another. We can get also get angry on top of our depression, because we think that we shouldn't experience depression, that we should always be happy in life.

Lost opportunities—all those "would'ves, could'ves, and should'ves" in life—can be a source of depression. Depression is really prevalent among individuals recovering from an addiction—to drugs, food, alcohol, and so forth. They have lost relationships, jobs, opportunties, and life experiences, and so they have to deal not only with the phsyical and mental pressures of staying sober, but also with the discouragement and depression having lost so many things in their lives. In a similar sense, we all have lost things in our lives. We are all in recovery—recovery from hurt, pain, or just an unfufilled life—and this loss makes us experience depression.

What is a midlife crisis? It's simply when you reflect over your past and realize what you don't have or what you have lost. This assessment can happen any time in the circle of life; it is a survey of where you are now, with the conclusion that you are not where you are supposed to be, that your life is not living up to your expectations. Some people in the midst of a midlife crisis make those clichéd changes—they get divorced, run off with their secretary, and buy a red sportscar. Others stay in a state of depression and hopelessness, feeling like nothing will ever change. They feel that their loss cannot be overcome and that they are doomed for the rest of their lives.

I would like to make a simple suggestion for dealing with depression. It's difficult to do but can be life-changing: be grateful for what you do have. Make a list of the good things in your life, even the simplest things, and be thankful. Focus your thoughts on what you do have and not what you do not have.

If you change the way you think, you will change the way you feel.

That's easy to say, of course, but it can be difficult to stay with the new you until it becomes part of you. Think of what kind of person you would like to be: happy and grateful or sad and depressed. Choose to be happy and grateful. Now make that list.

In his book *Psycho-Cybernectics*, plastic surgeon Dr. Maxwell Maltz says it takes twenty-one days to form a new habit. This statement was based on his observations of operating on patients and seeing how long it took them to adjust to their new faces. Try to be positive every day for twenty-one days, and see and feel the difference in your emotions. Phillppa

Lally, a researcher at University College London, published a study in the *European Journal of Social Psychology* concluding that it takes sixty-six days for a habit to become automatic. So it takes a least twenty-one days to form a habit and a good sixty-six days to make it stick. A couple of months is a short amount of time to invest in the making of a new you.

I know that some depression and anxiety can be organic, resulting from a chemical imbalance or a brain-related injury that needs medical assistance. If this is the case with you, work on changing your thoughts to go along with any help you get from medications.

Chapter 7

Anxiety

I would like to talk about anxiety. There are many good books on this subject, and I cannot pretend to come close to their depth of understanding. But hear me out. The definition of anxiety, according to Merriam-Webster, is "painful or apprehensive uneasiness of mind, usually over an impending or anticipated ill."

Simply put, anxiety is the anticipation of an unpleasant future event.

Some people feel anxiety about going to the dentist. Others are worried and anxious about something in the near or distant future that they do not want to confront or experience. And again, we can experience anger, layering it on top of our anxiety, because we don't like feeling anxiety and think we should be free of it. We get mad at ourselves for being anxious. We know that we shouldn't be anxious, and we hate the feeling of anxiety and the physical symptoms that accompany it.

Accepting anxiety is a great step toward making it through those feelings. It is okay to feel the emotion of anxiety because you are anticipating a future event that may be unpleasant. Don't be hard on yourself. Accept your feelings and move on, and try to replace those anxious thoughts with pleasant thoughts or memories.

On the other side of the coin, there is a good form of anxiety, like anticipating your Friday paycheck. The good form of anxiety can be motivation to prepare for that upcoming event. If you are a musician, an upcoming concert can cause anxiety. This anxiety will be a cue to prepare or practice more.

But mostly we think of anxiety as something negative. What is strange about anxiety is that we can be bent out of shape with the anticipation of an unpleasant experience in the future, but we can also be anxious simply about being anxious, with no unpleasant event on our minds. Anxiety can be like a black cloud coming out of nowhere. Being anxious about being anxious is a weird twist in the human psyche. Some people experience anxiety attacks that bring on physical symptoms such as a rapid heartbeat, a dry mouth, and profuse sweating. They may not have any anxious thoughts, but because their physical symptoms seemed to appear out of nowhere, they experience an anxiety attack—and because of this, they are afraid of having a future attack. They are having an anxiety attack because they are anticipating the unpleasant future event of another anxiety attack.

One funny thing about the future is that it doesn't always happen the way we think it will. That is, we can be anxious for nothing. One trick to stop worrying about the future is to live in the moment, to postpone worrying about tomorrow until tomorrow. There is nothing wrong with thinking about the future, planning for it and rehearsing for it, but anxiety takes thinking to the next level; it becomes extreme. Anxiety is a constant flow of thoughts, often the same ones over and over and over. You get to the point that it's like you're on a merry-go-round that you can't get off. This is called obsessive-complusive thinking, when we think the same thoughts over and over and over again. According to the National Alliance of Mental Illness, those thoughts are sometimes accompanied by rituals to provide some momentary relief—for example, washing the hands to alleviate the fear of germs, or checking and rechecking the locks on doors to alleviate the fear of intruders.

Anxiety can have a medical cause as well. A sense of gloom, heaviness, despair, and anxiety that appears out of the clear blue sky could be attributed to chemical or hormonal imbalances. Medications can be helpful in such cases.

Anxiety is crazy and hard to beat, but it can be done. I am one of many people who have experienced anxiety or panic attacks. I know from experience that having an anxiety attack over the anticipation of having an anxiety attack is real and common.

It's crazy how the mind works. My suggestion for relieving panic attacks related to physical symptoms is to understand that those symptoms can be caused by some physiological trigger you're not even aware of—maybe even a food you just ate. Just because your heart is racing doesn't mean you are going to have anxiety attached to that symptom. Also, try going to your happy place to displace the thought of unwanted thoughts. Distract your mind in some way to take its focus off the unwanted future event. Think thoughts that bring you pleasant feelings. Try to think in as much detail as possible, with colors, sounds, textures, and such.

If you are anxious, it may be because you are anticipating some unpleasant event in the near future and you are worried about it. (Remember, what your mind perceives to be true is true to you.) Another way to cope with anxiety is to be open to the possibility that the future event may not be as bad as you think—and even if it is, you will survive and move on. Put the future event into its proper place. Don't blow it out of proportion. Don't make a mountain out of a molehill. Going to the dentist may be uncomfortable, but you'll reap the benefit of better health.

To overcome these panic attacks, therefore, you have to displace your anxious thoughts, replacing them with new thoughts that make you feel different. See the next chapter on the Displacement Principle.

Chapter 8

The Replacement, Displacement Principle

Getting Rid of Unpleasant Thoughts

Displacing negative thoughts, which make us feel bad, with positive thoughts, which make us feel good about ourselves, is the key to changing our feelings. It is difficult to stop thinking about something entirely; you have to displace the thought. So why not displace the negative thoughts with positive thoughts that will have the benefit of making you feel better about yourself and life in general? Keep in mind that it takes practice and patience. You didn't get to where you are now overnight, and so it will take some time to feel the change. And as you go through new stages in life, you will find new opportunites to work on your thinking.

May I suggest that the moment you find yourself on a mental merry-go-round (when you are thinking the same thoughts over and over, without any new or different information), make a decision to displace those thoughts. Learn to recognize the signs when you step on the merry-go-round, and then switch your thoughts as soon as possible.

Your mind, like your body, needs rest, so take a mental vacation. Go to a happy place. Think of its sights, sounds, colors, and smells in as much detail as you can, and before you know it, you will not be angry or anxious anymore. Think of your favorite vacation or fishing spot; think of something that you can stay focused on and that will bring good memories and good feelings. It is a form of daydreaming, but with purpose.

Another way of displacing your negative thoughts is simply to focus on your breathing. Concentrate on the sensation of air coming into your lungs and then blowing out. Focus on how cool and fresh the air is, and the life that each breath brings, and then focus on the warmth and the release of toxins and tension as your breath exits your lungs.

There are many other stress-reduction exercises, and plenty of books and articles and vidoes on the subject online, so find the right ones for you. Practicing them before you need them is the key. Practice going to your happy place before a crisis hits, and just like muscle memory, the brain will be easier to control when you need it most.

In one form of displacement therapy, the patient is taught to wear a rubber band around his or her wrist and snap it against the skin to combat anxious thoughts. An article in *Psychology Today* entitled "Unwanted Thoughts? Snap the Rubber Band" suggests defusing a negative thought by addressing it directly, talking to it and calling it silly. In his book *Don't Panic*, Reid Wilson, PhD, suggests saying the word *stop* out loud to stop the obsessive thinking. The pain of the rubber band and the word *stop* said out loud interrupt the thought process. The whole idea is to replace and displace your thoughts. Then, after the snap, think of something pleasant. Your brain will be refreshed, and you just may have a different perspective or a solution.

This is part of life's journey, experiencing emotions from our thoughts. We need to embrace it as part of being human.

It is okay to feel—to feel anything!

Our challenge is to respond to our emotions not with a knee-jerk reaction, but with self-control and confidence. We should decide how to respond. We should make that choice and not react in an out-of-control way. Reacting to our emotions is usually what gets us into trouble. That's why we so often hear people say, "I didn't know what I was doing, I was so upset and so angry."

We often make excuses for our behavior by blaming it on some emotion that was out of control. But the truth is, we all have a choice in how we respond. It might be that our poor choices and responses earlier in life have now become habitual, done without much thinking involved. These responses have become so automatic that we don't think about the consequences until it is too late.

Before I end my thoughts on this subject, let me say that I know anxiety sometimes floods our minds and bodies with seemingly no invitation from us. It can occur in the middle of the night or day, for no apparent reason; our thoughts at the time seem to have no direct connection to the panic attack. My advice on this subject is not intended to replace professional help, and we are still learning much about what causes anxiety or panic attacks. Even so, you can work on the rational side of your thoughts and become more positive and grateful during those attacks, reassuring yourself that this too shall pass. Hang in there.

Chapter 9

My Relationships Make Me Angry

The Stronger the Relationship, the More Intense the Anger

When there is tension between two people, the depth of their relationship is directly proportional to the intensity and duration of their anger. The point here is that the type of relationship determines the intensity and duration of anger from unmet expectations. The people who are closest to us are the ones who can push our buttons more quickly and easily than anyone (more than someone walking by on the street, for example). Of course, in human behavior there are always exceptions to the rule.

We can still get angry at someone we barely know, but the intensity and duration of our anger is not likely to last as long as it would if we were angry at someone close to us. It's our spouse, father, mother, brother, sister, coworker, or boss who can really make us mad, because we have stronger and deeper expectations for them. ("She should respect me because she is my wife." "He should accept me for who I am because he is my brother.") We feel that these people should respect us and love us. We feel that they should keep their word. Our "should/should not" list can be unlimited where they are concerned. We have fewer and less intense expectations of people we barely know.

If you walk into a room and your eyes meet those of someone new, you'll probably smile and acknowledge him. According to social norms, he should respond to you with a smile or some other form of acknowledgment. Now, if he turns his head away from your glance and ignores your smile, you could get a little peeved, thinking that he is impolite and snobbish. You might be put off, but usually you'll move on and let it go, unless this is a scenario repeated often in your life. In this situation, there is very little depth to the relationship in question, and so you may not feel as intensely as you would if you knew the person and he treated you coldly by design.

To keep from getting really angry, you can change your expectation from "Everyone should be polite" to "Not everyone is polite or capable of being polite." Also, you can minimize the slight in your own head by thinking that the impolite person is the one missing out on being in a relationship with you.

In our society, we have expectations centered around the social courtesies that we (or most of us) learned during childhood. Acknowledging people when you meet them or when they enter the room is one of them. In the above example, we changed our expectation to recognize that some inconsiderate people will not follow all the social courtesies. We did this to keep from going insane. If we say hi to people, we expect them to be polite and say hi back. But on the rare occasions when people do not respond or are impolite, we won't be so miffed if we have modified our expectations to accept people who do not share our social expectations.

I don't know about you, but I feel that my expectations are reasonable; otherwise, why would I have them? We only get angry when our reasonable expectations are not met. One of the ways to manage your anger is to look at the expectation involved and challenge your thinking: *Is this really a reasonable expectation? Should I modify it to make it more reasonable?* Try asking someone else about your expectation: either he will confirm that it is reasonable (he has it too), or he will say, "You're crazy—you shouldn't expect that." There may be some wisdom in acknowledging the "crazy" part in your life. Just on the inside bet, your expectation may be unreasonable. If you are open to the possibility that you're wrong, the intensity of your anger will drop and your response will be more in line with what is acceptable. That will keep you out of trouble.

A good example is driving, and the anger many of us feel when our expectations aren't met out on the road. We tend to feel that everyone should drive the way we do: professionally, courteously, and skillfully. If they did, there wouldn't be any traffic problems!

We make judgments and evaluate other people's driving, sometimes thinking they shouldn't even be on the road. However, when we cut someone off, change lanes without using our turn signal, or weave in and out of traffic, we are doing so because we are skillful drivers—not like those idiots who need to go back to driver's ed.

What if we modified our expectations of how others should drive, changing them to something more reasonable? How about changing our thinking to assume that there are many drivers on the road, with many different skill levels and abilities? How about recognizing that we *all* make mistakes on the road? Maybe we should have a little more tolerance for others; after all, our driving records are not perfect, yet we tolerate our own driving.

We would all be less-angry drivers if we simply modified our expectations to allow for less-than-stellar driving by others. As a matter of fact, if we expected to encounter drivers with different skill levels, our expectations would actually be met, and we would be not angry, but happy! (Just kidding. Maybe not happy, but at least not consumed with road rage. Wouldn't that be nice?)

In summary, we know that the people closest to us can make us the angriest, and because we think our expectations are right, we may need to modify those expectations to include people who do not live up to them.

Chapter 10

Global Anger

Waking Up in a Bad Mood, Mad at the World

Some of us just seem to wake up in a bad mood, already feeling angry. We don't know the specific unmet expectations that are making us angry, but we know that we are not looking forward to the day. Life overall is not going our way.

If we are not happy with the direction of our lives, we can wake up angry each morning and be unhappy all day. When we are unhappy with our job, with our marriage, with our children, with our church, with society in general, or even (dare I say it) with God, we can wake up in the morning feeling angry, frustrated, and not motivated to look for anything positive in our lives. We feel justified in feeling bad, and we don't want to cede that position. Anger actually becomes our friend, and eventually we lose touch with the moments of pleasure and happiness that surround us. We lose sight of the things we should be grateful for.

If you are in this place, take a moment to reflect on what kind of person you want to be. Please know that you didn't get to this place overnight, and you can start to take small steps to becoming happier and more at peace with the world around you. This may sound trite and too simple, but seriously, think about being thankful for what you do have. Think about what makes you happy. Know that your thoughts directly affect the way you feel.

You think ⟶ You feel ⟶ You act

Just a side note here: research is confirming over and over that happy people tend to be grateful people, and that they are healthier than unhappy people. (See research by the Center for Advancement of Health, "Happiness and Satisfaction Might Lead to Better Health," published in the September 2, 2008, edition of *Science Daily*.) These people also end up expressing their gratitude to others. Try gratitude and see if it works for you.

If you are feeling something negative, ask yourself, *What am I thinking to cause these feelings?* If you have lost something important—a job, a loved one, an opportunity—then you are most likely feeling depressed. If you generally feel lost in life with no plan or purpose, you will struggle with depression. Apart from any chemical imbalance in your brain, what you think affects the way you feel.

In teaching anger management seminars to people who struggle with addiction, people who have in many cases lost everything, I've found that they have deep anger toward themselves and those around them. Life has not met their expectations; things haven't turned out the way they "should have." I call this "global anger." It is a fact that some people are just not happy with life. They are angry most of the time because they think life is not going their way.

Focusing on unmet expectations and desires, and things that should or should not have happened, will make anyone angry and unhappy. Global anger lumps everything together, overriding any positives. It concludes that "my life sucks." If this is you, hang in there; there is hope for all of us on this journey. Please take a moment and make a list of things that you do have that are positive. It may start simply with the fact that you are breathing. Focus on the fact that you have a purpose in this life, that you have value and worth, and that we are going to find them together. Work on being thankful, and I guarantee that you will be much happier and a better person for it.

Chapter 11

Venting

The subject of venting anger is an interesting one. If you believe venting works and is necessary for you to feel better, then it works. But in reality, venting your anger (getting things off your chest, letting it all hang out, blowing off steam) coincides with the body and mind's natural process of arousal and depletion of energy—that is, the increase of energy from the release of hormones and the natural decline after the hormones wear off. According to research published in the February 2013 edition of *Cyberpsychology, Behavior, and Social Networking,* when people read and write rants online, they experience a negative mood shift. Martin RC of the Human Development Dept of University of Wisconsin publish a study (Cyberpsychol Behav Soc. NETW 2013 Feb:16 119—122)

People mistake the "downhill" feeling of releasing pent-up anger as confirmation that it works, that it is necessary to prevent them from blowing up in an even worse way later. Venting feels good because our bodies go through a natural depletion of energy, and we mistake that feeling for working out our anger.

Another reason people blow up when they are angry is that it works—they get their way. Most people will yield to someone who displays anger openly and aggressively.

Basically they'll give in, saying, "If you are really that upset, then go ahead and have it your way," or something similar to that. Then what they have done is reinforced that person's behavior, and the cycle is repeated: get angry and you get what you want. If we allow angry people to get their way, they will repeat their behavior because it works.

For the angry person, this display of anger is usually lopsided, over the top. For the most part, that person has little regard or respect for the object of his anger. Otherwise, he wouldn't act inappropriate or be disrespectful.

When someone displays anger appropriately, he shows self-control and respect toward the object of his anger. Then there is an opportunity to resolve the conflict.

Respect is the key.

When people are angry at each other, or feeling some other negative emotion toward each other, but also treat each other with respect, their messages are more likely to be received and heard. But when people are disrespectful toward each other, it will be very difficult, if not impossible, for them to resolve the issue. They can't listen to the issues if they feel disrespected. The issue switches to how things are said rather than whatever problem started the discussion, and they have to sort through the issue of disrespect before returning to the initial complaint. If respect is shown on both sides, then there is more of a chance to work through the issues.

It is the "tempest in a teapot" theory—the concept that there's some reservoir of energy, some force stored somewhere in the body or mind, that must be released in order to prevent future harm, just like steam must be released from a teapot so it doesn't explode. The idea is similar to the old adage about the straw that breaks the camel's back. We can work ourselves into believing that we can't take it anymore, that our reservoir is full, that this is the last straw. Then we blow up.

To my knowledge, research has failed to find any physical location in the brain or elsewhere that holds any water with that theory (pun intended). At what point, at what level, do we mark that reservoir full and ready to overflow? How can we measure when it is full enough? It can't be done. It is a subjective perception held by the individual. *I have to vent, or I am going to blow up.* This thought is subjective. It cannot be measured, weighed, or put in a box, but it is very real to the person who thinks it. One's perception is one's reality.

The mind is an amazing organ. What we perceive to be true is true to us. Therefore, if you perceive that venting is necessary for your mental health, then it will be. But I would like to challenge your perspective on this. Why is it that two people can experience the same offense and one can handle it and the other can't (full reservoir)? My answer to that is, we are what we think. So if it is true to you, then it is true. That so-called reservoir has no limit to its capacity, only the one we give it.

What about the idea of confessing our anger to someone as a way of venting? Isn't this healthy? Yes, maybe. Confessing can be good or bad; it depends. Confessing can be of value if you are not attacking the object of your anger, but simply sharing your anger with someone else who has an ear to hear. This can be a healthy way of listening to your own words. Sometimes when we speak out loud, we hear how foolish we sound or hear the answer as we speak. Then, ideally, we'll be open to the suggestions of the one who is listening, or we'll feel the healing power of that person's empathy toward us.

· Confessing can have both good and bad results. First the good result: if you confess your problem to someone and then feel empathy and understanding in return, and this is all you need or expect, then you will feel better. You may feel some physical or mental change, perhaps a sense of relief through your confession, because you have received affirmation, understanding, and possibly some input to help you handle or resolve the situation. Venting worked. You got it off your chest, and now you feel better.

On the other hand, venting doesn't always work. Confession can make you relive the negative emotions and feelings all over again. When you share the story of what made you mad, the adrenaline can begin to flow just as it did when the initial offense occurred, and you can get angry all over again. You could be sitting with some friends, listening and talking about everyone's day, with no intention of getting angry, but then as you begin to tell them about your day and all the events that made you mad, you become boiling mad.

Confessions, more often than not, rehearse the anger in your mind. This rehearsal can release the hormones famous for creating the "fight or flight" response, making you angry all over again. Be careful about your reasons and motivation when you discuss things that make you mad, as they can make you mad in the moment all over again.

Along with the reservoir theory is the repression theory—a similar concept, with the difference being that, in this case, you are angry and don't know it. Anger is deep inside your unconscious, waiting to get out. Something in your past, something you may or may not remember, has deposited anger there, and now the anger is waiting for release. And if the anger doesn't get out, it may erupt like a volcano at another date and time. This repressed anger has something in common with the Loch Ness Monster: we may believe it is there, but there is no way to prove its existence. How do you prove that something's not there? It is impossible.

Venting is akin to catharsis, the medical bloodletting of ancient times. Practiced for thousands of years, it stemmed from the idea that if someone was sick or had some emotional or spiritual malaise, a physician should cut the individual to let out some of the bad blood. The first president of the

United States, George Washington, had a common cold and the doctors let out too much blood, and he died from this medical procedure of catharsis. Ventilation and confession can have similar consequences, causing death to relationships with friends, family members, and coworkers if not done properly. See Knox, J. H Masn Jr. "The Medical History of George Washington, His physicians, Friends and Advisors." *Bulletin of the Institute of History of Medicine,* 1(1922), 174-91.

So now you know that ventilation really doesn't work. You will have to find another way to manage your anger. Anger management is all about self-control and learning the appropriate expression of anger at a given time and place.

Chapter 12

Pet Peeves

Things That Annoy You

Have you ever wondered why some of the things people say and do annoy you? They can be little things, like tapping their fingernails on a desk, snorting, talking with their mouth full, eating with their head two inches from their plate, not saying thanks after receiving a gift or kind gesture, squeezing the toothpaste from the middle, leaving the toilet seat up, leaving drawers open, not using the car's turn signals, constantly interrupting others, picking their nose, exaggerating everything, whining and complaining ... These are just a few samples of pet peeves. The list goes to infinity and beyond.

Again, all these pet peeves can be explained by the fact that we have expectations about how people should behave. Even though we recognize that these infractions are small compared to others, we can become very agitated over these unmet rules (expectations) of behavior. The more we're exposed to our pet peeves, such as an increased frequency and duration of these behaviors, the more annoyed we will be. It is easy to put up with someone else's quirky behavior if we don't have to be around it much—we may even think it's funny—but it would be a different story if we had to live with it. Being constantly exposed to our pet peeves keeps our nerves raw. It can drive us crazy.

What's the solution? How should we approach a minor problem that gets blown out of proportion? It is a matter of perspective.

Major in the major things in your life, and minor in the minor things.

I know that in the moment, doing so may be difficult. But you can practice beforehand, through visualization, before you are exposed to the pet peeve again. You probably already know this, but most musicians and athletes can practice their music or sports in their minds, without their instrument or equipment. Visualization is a powerful tool; much has been researched and written on the topic. Take advantage of this tool: pick something that annoys you and practice telling yourself that it doesn't bother you at all. As a matter of fact, you can look at this particular annoyance objectively and see it for what it is: no skin off your nose. This pet peeve won't matter to you an hour from now or a week from now. It really isn't all that important, and certainly it's not worth the energy to get all worked up about it.

Now that you are working on your pet peeves, try expanding the visualization technique to include the major sources of your anger. You will be surprised how well the technique works. Rehearse what makes you mad, and then rehearse how you want to respond or not respond. You can practice your response well in advance of the next time. Your response will get better over time and with practice.

Another reason we get mad over simple things is that they tend to happen repeatedly over time. So an incident may be small in itself, but after it happens to us over and over, we finally get angry and hostile about it. As a result, we might focus our anger on some unsuspecting individual who is clueless about why we are so angry. We must try to keep everything in perspective: major in the major things in life, and minor in the minor things.

Chapter 13

Forgiveness

The Spiritual Side of Anger Management

What does forgiveness mean to you? Forgetting the event? Forgetting the reason that you were mad? I think there is more to forgiveness than just forgetting. I think you can forgive and not forget. Some things you can never forget, but you can forgive.

Let me explain. I put on seminars for people fighting addiction. Many of them come to my class having destroyed their relationships with their wives, parents, families, and friends. As part of their recovery, many of them will seek reconciliation with the people they have wronged. In the process, they usually ask for forgiveness from those people. They are not asking people to forget what they have done; they're simply asking for forgiveness, and to be treated in a different way. For those who have been wronged, it can be very difficult to forgive, especially if the person isn't asking their forgiveness for the first time. Here is my definition of forgiveness:

Forgiveness is releasing the object of your anger from any consequences of your anger.

Bear with me a moment as I explain. Forgiveness is not forgetting, but simply treating the object of your anger as if the offense never happened. That is true forgiveness. It can be extended each time the offense is brought to mind. In many cases, this is exactly what happens.

The Forgiveness Cycle

First we forgive someone, ➡ then we remember the offense, ➡ then we feel angry and hurt again, ➡ and then we need to forgive again, releasing that person from the consequences of our anger.

This process is not easy, and it takes time, but it gets easier as time passes. We can still be hurt, upset, and angry, but we need to treat the offender as if the offense never happened. We can still feel the emotion of anger, but the act of forgiveness means treating the person as if it never happened, even when we still feel anger.

More often than not, we'll say we forgive people but then remind them of their past offenses at the first opportunity, especially if there is any hint that they've messed up again. If we've really forgiven them, we'll put the past behind us, along with our desire to punish the offenders by reminding them of their offense.

First we must treat them as if they never committed the offense (our behavior response), and then we must look in our hearts to find the desire to do the same (our spiritual response). It is very much like the saying in addicts' circles: "Fake it till you make it." When you ask people to forgive you, you are not really asking them to forget what happened, but to treat you as they would if the offense had never happened—to quit bringing it up and throwing it in your face whenever there is an opportunity.

There's a difference. Forgiveness is difficult but very rewarding. It is the spiritual aspect of anger management. It really leads to the path of inner peace and lays the groundwork for peace with others. I've found that forgiveness is the key to freedom for many people who attend my seminars. One gentleman came up to me after a session on forgiveness and was visibly crying. He shared with me that his wife of thirty years had died of cancer three years earlier and he was angry with her doctors. That day, after hearing my talk about forgiveness, he forgave them—and he was freed from his prison of hate and anger. I have seen it over and over: those who struggle with addiction, those who have been in and out of prison, those who are angry with their past, those who have grown up with disappointments on every corner, those who have been treated unfairly, learning to forgive and finding peace for the first time in their lives.

Many individuals fighting addiction and anger have attended mandatory anger management sessions or classes, in and out of prison, but they have never heard about the spiritual aspect of forgiveness as it relates to anger. You should see the expression of freedom on their faces when they learn to forgive people in their past and present. We can even forgive people who are no longer with us. We can forgive people who haven't asked us for forgiveness. We can forgive a parent who has died. We can forgive society for our mistreatment and for the unfair system we've experienced.

Forgiveness is the greatest tool we can have in dealing with anger. We can choose daily to forgive all our grievances resulting from unmet expectations. Turning anger into forgiveness can be the most radical transformation of your life. It will change you from an unhappy, self-centered individual to an individual whose sense of freedom defies description. Walking in forgiveness is amazing and so life-changing. It allows us to live in the moment, treasuring each and every breath. It is not easy, but it is worth the effort.

This is the most important subject in this book—the spiritual aspect of anger management. I wanted to make it the first chapter, but I felt that I needed to lay some groundwork first.

We should walk and live in forgiveness.

We can't spend every moment of the day trying to work through our issues as well as everyone else's. That would be emotional hell. We need to pick and choose what is important to us and to those around us, which issues will strengthen our relationships rather than dividing, and work on those.

Ask yourself, If I bring up this issue that makes me angry, is it good for me (or us), or will it cause more harm? If it causes harm, it might be a long time before everyone gets over the particular issue and the way it was handled.

Chapter 14

Self-Esteem

What we perceive to be true is true for us. Our self-esteem is defined in terms of how we perceive, esteem, or value ourselves. The word *esteem* basically means to value, to place worth. So how do we value ourselves, especially in comparison to others?

If we think of ourselves as more valuable and important than others, we will have an inflated sense of self-esteem and will tend to be more openly aggressive, verbally and physically, with our anger. Why? Because our goal is to communicate that we are angry; therefore, we put less emphasis on other people's feelings and treat those people with less respect. In our minds, our feelings are more important than the feelings of the people we're angry with. The following chapter on social styles explains how our personality and self-esteem influence our expression of anger.

On the other hand, if we think of ourselves as less important than others, we will have the tendency not to speak up or express our feelings. That is because we do not want to rock the boat and cause waves that are uncomfortable. We will tend to suck up our feelings for the sake of keeping the peace. We will suppress our anger in most situations, pretending that it is not there.

Then on rare occasions we will explode in rage. Why? Because we are not good at sharing our feelings, and we haven't learned the benefit of sharing them on a smaller scale. When we just can't take it anymore, we blow up. People will wonder where that anger came from, because they haven't seen it before. Those of us who struggle with low self-esteem need to learn that it is okay to express our feelings in an appropriate setting.

Finding balance in our self-esteem and its effects on our response to anger means realizing that we have value and worth, but so do others, and that when we share our uncomfortable feelings of anger, we must do so with respect for others.

These are the keys to displaying anger appropriately: value and respect.

If we respect and value the object of our anger, we will be more likely to set the stage for working through the situation.

Now, we know that most people don't like to be criticized or told that they've made us or others angry. So we need to evaluate the situation and determine whether what we are sharing will produce the desired response from the other person. Let's be truthful: most of the time it will not. When we share our anger, most people do not know how to handle it. We do not live in a culture in which we have role models to show us how to appropriately display and respond to anger.

In our culture, if you share that you are mad with someone, that person will respond with anger. He or she will be mad at you regardless of the legitimacy of your anger. It makes us mad when people are mad at us, regardless of the reason.

This response is really prominent among men. Most women grew up playing house or other role-play games that helped them learn to sort through their emotions. This skill is helpful later in life.

Men, on the other hand, played games that are aggressive and violent. Think about that for a moment. Men as a whole do not have role models in real day-to-day life, the entertainment arena, or even in most spiritual settings who demonstrate talking about deep and sensitive feelings. Sharing negative emotions in a respectful way is often missing in the male formula. Most TV sitcoms and movies make fun of men who display emotions that way.

We know that there is a time and place to share, and we need to learn to be better with our timing. We can't live in a society where everyone talks about his or her feelings all day long. Can you imagine a world where everyone did that? Maybe you know someone who does this. Or maybe it is you. For most of us, too much sharing is TMI: too much information.

If you tend to share your feelings a lot, you will notice that people tend to pull away from you, except for people like you. There is a social game in every culture that has to do with how much you should say about yourself. It is called "the art of disclosure." You say a little about yourself and then pass the baton to the other person, who then has a chance to respond. If that person shares a little about herself and gives an indication that she wants more from you, you respond back.

Some people are clueless about this social game and share information about their feelings, problems, body aches, and so forth, without listening or watching for clues that the other person is or is not interested. So if you have the tendency to dominate the conversation, cut back and work on asking others questions that show you are interested in them as well. You will be amazed to discover that people's favorite subject is themselves—and it doesn't take much to get them to talk about it.

Saying hi is all some people want from you. They are not really interested in your day or your problems. If you continue to share, they will eventually stop the conversation, make an excuse, and leave the room. You might have noticed others who've made a similar escape when you first entered a room. All some people want is to say hi, and so they'll extend that social courtesy to you. They do not want to listen to you talk about all your problems. If you are that person, please do not get offended; it is just that most people are not like you. It is not a matter of right or wrong—just different. When you find someone like you, think of it is a great blessing that you should treasure as such.

Listen and watch for verbal clues to see if people are interested in your ideas and feelings. You will be surprised by how many times they will listen and respond, but give them some say in the timing of that conversation. If you dominate the conversation, they will find an excuse to leave the room or hang up the phone. All of us want to talk about ourselves if we have someone to listen. Ask people questions about themselves and let them talk, and perhaps the baton will be passed back to you. Then watch your relationship grow.

Whew! I hope that helps. Remember, what we perceive as real is our reality. Can we all work on respecting others? Whether we have too much self-esteem, valuing ourselves more than others, or low self-esteem, valuing ourselves less than others, respect goes a long way in resolving conflicts in relationships.

Chapter 15

How to Deal with an Angry Person

When I first started my anger management seminars, I didn't approach this subject, because it was a seminar for people dealing with their own anger issues. But I was asked about this issue so often that I added the subject to the seminar. Most people I encounter are quick to say that they don't have an anger problem—but boy, do they know someone who really does. We all have to deal with our own issues, but what do we do when others are angry at us? I hope the following information will be of some help to you.

The first step is the most obvious but sometimes the most difficult too: don't escalate the situation. In other words, stay in control and do not add to fuel to the fire that is making the other person angry.

After a fight or argument, the issues that started the whole thing are sometimes forgotten. What stains the memory is how the fight or argument played out. It is often how you fight that escalates the heat of the argument on both sides. So if possible, watch how you come across. Make sure not to add any more heat to the argument. Do your best to defuse the level of intensity, creating the opportunity to calmly and respectfully work through the issue.

If you can, meet in a neutral place if you know the subject matter is going to provoke strong feelings. I would suggest a corner booth in a restaurant—someplace where the conversation will be private but the public setting will help keep both parties on task and their behavior restrained.

Again, the number one issue is respect. If you are the person who is angry and you want to communicate that anger to someone, do it in such a way that demonstrates that you still respect that person. Make your complaints specific to the behavior, event, or problem that makes you angry; do not attack the person's character. Remember, it is the specific situation that has made you mad. Attacking someone's character and disrespecting him will not resolve the issue.

Example: Instead of calling a person rude, self-centered, or disrespectful because she didn't return your text, tell her that you felt hurt and of little value when she repeatedly ignored your texts and phone calls. Focus on "I" statements, not statements attacking the other person.

Communicating hatred toward that person in the heat of the moment will not be productive. You may get your point across, but most likely the damage done to the relationship will take a long to time to repair, if it can be repaired.

If you are the person on the receiving end of the anger, the same rule is applicable to you. Showing respect in this situation can be difficult, because you are under attack and you may feel angry for being disrespected yourself. But hang in there, stay above the fray, and demonstrate that you are in control and can respect the other person, even when he or she temporarily doesn't deserve it and has disrespected you. Take the higher road. By doing so, you will help cool down the temperature of the angry person.

Angry people want to be heard. That is why so many times they are out of control—because they feel they are not being listened to unless they yell and scream. So listen to them, demonstrate that you value them, give them a chance to speak, and then respond. Try repeating back or rephrasing their complaint and then asking them if you got it right. Then ask for permission to respond to their complaint.

Understand why angry people are in the habit of displaying their anger: because it works. They get their way when they display anger. They want you to know that they are angry, and they want things their way.

Their displays of anger work because most people do not like conflict and will let angry people have their way in order to make them go away. And when authority figures display their anger, many people are afraid to confront them for fear of losing their jobs or some other negative repercussions. So in general, angry people act angry because they get what they want when they do.

The second step is affirming the angry person's feelings without agreeing with her perspective. As I mentioned before, you can listen to her and rephrase why she is angry, and then ask her if what you just said is correct. This is called reflective conversation. It lets her know you are listening.

For example, I might rephrase to you your angry complaint with me: "You are angry with me because I didn't call you back," or "You're upset because I was late for dinner," or "What I said at the barbecue hurt your feelings." With these statements, I'm restating to you what I believe is making you angry before I respond with my defense or comments.

You get the picture. It takes a little practice, but active listening can tone down the heat of other people's anger tremendously. Often they will calm down just because you are really listening to them and seem to understand.

Sometimes, asking questions about their anger and the reasons for it will lower the intensity of their anger. Before responding with your comments, justifications, or explanations, demonstrate that you are really trying to understand them. After getting a good handle on why they are angry, respectfully ask them for permission to share your thoughts and feelings, setting the stage for back-and-forth, productive conversation. You gave them their turn, and now it is your turn, and you are asking them to give you the same respect and patience during your response.

The trick is to wait and listen. When asking questions, show patience and restraint until it is your turn to respond to their issue. You may again need to ask permission to have a turn to respond. If you jump in and argue your case before listening to them, most likely you will end up yelling over each other, and no one will really be listening. In that case, the person who yells the most or the loudest will feel like the winner, but in fact, nobody will win. One of you may get your way, but the relationship is the loser.

So when there is a break in the conversation and the other person seems ready to hear what you have to say, address the issue by first apologizing, saying something like "I have made you angry, and I would like to work this out." Maybe ask the person whether they want to work things out as well. If you are at fault, ask for their forgiveness, and then ask for any suggestions that may help you change your behavior or the way you come across.

If you are not at fault, start out by telling them you're sorry that they feel hurt and angry, and then state calmly, for the record, that you have a different view of the situation— that you never intended to come across that way to them, that they misunderstood or misinterpreted what you said, texted, or e-mailed to them, etc. If they seem to be cooling down, ask them for permission to explain yourself.

It might sound silly, but asking for permission to speak throughout the conversation allows both of you to gather your thoughts and prepare your response. If possible, ask questions. This communicates to them that you are listening to and affirming her. This approach can be very difficult at first, and you won't find it modeled anywhere in life, especially not on TV or in movies. This kind of interaction would not make a good movie or sitcom, but it makes for a good relationship. Think about it: in our society, we just don't have good role models for dealing with our own anger, and especially not for dealing with the anger of others.

You can affirm and respect the other person whether you agree or disagree with his perspective. Sometimes you will never see the issue the same way. If that is the case, ask if you can agree to disagree. The greater issue at stake here is your relationship with the other person. If it someone you really don't care about, then the effort and energy you're willing to spend to make things right will be limited. But on the other hand, our most intense arguments tend to be with those with whom we are close.

"Whatever is best for the relationship": Doesn't it make sense to have this as the foundational principle underlying your disagreement? Before engaging in an argument with someone you care about, ask yourself these questions: *Does this issue bring us closer together or drive us apart? Is this issue really worth the emotional drama and energy moving forward in the relationship?* I would hazard a guess that the majority of irritations in life that make us angry are really not that important, and in those cases we can make a conscious decision to drop the issue. So let it go. Forgive the object of your anger and move on.

The most important thing in life is relationships and the time spent enjoying them.

Chapter 16

The Morality of Anger

Right or Wrong?

Now let us address the morality of anger. In my seminars, I ask the participants whether they think anger is good or bad for you. I always get the same answers. Some people will say emphatically that anger is bad for you; others will say that it is good. It is a trick question. The answer that I am looking for is "It depends." Really, it does.

Your perspective is your reality. How you interpret a challenging social situation affects whether or not you get angry about it. Anger is a product of a social event combined with your specific genes and tendencies. Each culture has its own standards, its own shoulds and should nots, which are handed down through the generations. There are many similarities among the rules of various cultures, but there are some distinct differences as well.

Something that would make someone angry in one culture can be perfectly acceptable in another. I get a kick reading newspaper stories about American dignitaries making social gaffes in other countries. Their comments or gestures may be perfectly acceptable here in the States, but offensive in the country they are visiting. Whether our anger is good (justified) or bad (inappropriate) depends upon the culture or subculture that we live in.

Culture defines morality. Whether we learn it in church, from our parents, or from society, we learn what is right or wrong, especially when it comes to responding to the emotion of anger.

Some anger is good for you, and some anger is bad for you. Being angry about an injustice is "good" anger only if it is displayed in a way that is socially acceptable and responsible. Sometimes anger can be good if it motivates you to accomplish a goal. For an example, I might be so angry about my lack of money and my low-paying job that I decide to go to school to get a better job. That would be good anger. (I don't need to give you an example of bad anger; all you have to do is open a newspaper to read about people who were mad and responded in ways that hurt other people and things.)

Anger is an emotion. Emotions are neutral, neither good nor bad; they are just what we feel as humans. It is how we respond to our emotions that can get us into trouble.

Did you know that we can get into trouble from being too happy? Some people have been court ordered to come to my class because they were out celebrating and did something stupid. The judge didn't order them to "happiness management class"; no, the judge sent them to my anger management class. Why? Because the same principles that apply to anger apply to all our emotions. We think, we feel, and then we act. Emotions are neutral, but our response to them is judged by the culture that we live in. Anger management class should really be called "emotion management class." In other words, it is all about learning to behave with self-control.

In some cultures, if you are angry and demonstrate it, you lose face. You are punished for your lack of self-control. But in other cultures, you can lose face by not responding with a display of anger. You will be considered weak and shamed by others.

Many years ago in the United States, this used to be midwestern culture. If you were a man and angry, it was not only acceptable to respond verbally, but it was often considered justifiable to physically assault the man who made you mad. If the police showed up, they would tell everyone to cool down and go home and sleep it off. No one was punished for the public display of anger.

Today it is a different story. Responding with physical violence or verbal threats of violence against another person is not acceptable in our culture, except for very limited situations when someone is reasonably concerned about his safety or his life. Now you have to be careful about how you respond verbally, as you are judged by the aggressive words that come out of your mouth. Threatening someone can land you in jail.

In summary, our perspective affects how we interpret a situation, and the morality or appropriateness of our response is determined by the rules of the culture we live in.

Here are some questions to think about: Do you think anger is right or wrong? How does your opinion affect the way you react or respond to anger? In my seminars, I give everyone the right to be angry, the right to feel emotions, but not the right to display them any way they want to. It is okay to be angry, okay to be sad, okay to be depressed, okay to grieve, but the way we respond or react to those feelings might not be okay. Anger management is all about emotion management and self-control.

Chapter 17

Social Styles and Their Effects on Anger

How we respond or react to anger is learned. There may be a genetic component as well, but the overall, the way we react to anger is something we pick up from our parents and other family members, our friends, our culture, and media influences such as television. What we see and what they teach influences how we respond to anger. There may be some kind of genetic component that loads the gun, but it is what we learn from others that pulls the trigger. There may also be genetic differences between males and females that predispose them to respond to anger a certain way. But who knows, male and female responses to anger could be learned as well. As we know, learned anger responses can differ from society to society, from subculture to subculture. What is appropriate in one culture is not acceptable in another.

Can we change? Can we modify our behavior? Absolutely! Though we may be a sum product of our environment and our genetics, we can change. Believe it! Realizing that we have learned our anger responses will help us set the stage to learn and change. This chapter deals with understanding our basic tendencies and emotional responses.

There are four basic personalities or social styles that relate directly to how we respond to anger.

To identify your style, please fill out the following questionnaire, which contains ten simple sets of descriptions. For each set, choose the one that fits you best and then graph your answers according to the directions below the graph. Find the quadrants where your lines most often intersect. Then come back and read the rest of this chapter. Systema: *"The Sales of Relationship"* Systema Corportation Chicago, IL

Social Style Test

You use considerable body movement and/or use your hands freely	B-B or A-A	You are controlled, stiff, and/or have limited body movement
You tend to lean back, avoid face-to-face communication, make occasional eye contact	L-L or R-R	You tend to lean forward, face others squarely, hold constant eye contact
You are cool, distant, guarded in relationships	A-A or B-B	You are warm, friendly, emotional in relationships
Your speech is quick, fast-paced, strong, and/or demanding	R-R or L-L	Your speech is deliberate, slow-paced, quiet, and/or unassuming
You have unresponsive facial expressions, more of a "poker face"	A-A or B-B	You have responsive, animated facial expressions, smiling and frowning a lot
Your communication is to the point, clear, definitive	R-R or L-L	Your communication is vague and indefinite; you like to tell a story
Your viewpoints are open, expressing opinions with little emphasis on specific details	B-B or A-A	Your viewpoints are cautious and careful, with emphasis on facts and specific details
You use a moderate voice, make limited efforts to take a stand, leave situations unresolved	L-L or R-R	You use a moderate voice to emphasize points, take a stand, press for a decision
You are generally serious, thoughtful, and/or critical	A-A or B-B	You are mostly playful, fun-loving, joking around
Your facial expressions suggest a supportive, cooperative attitude	L-L or R-R	Your facial expressions suggest a dominant, competitive attitude

For each set of descriptions, look in the middle column and circle the two letters close to the description that best reflects you. There are no right or wrong answers. Try not to get stuck; pick the description that best represents the way you relate to others.

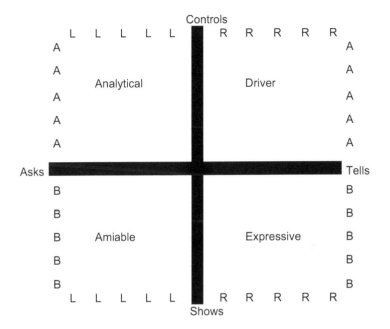

Using your answers from the previous page, connect the two letters for each answer, starting at the center of the graph and working your way toward the top, bottom, left, or right edge. See the examples on the next page to get started. You should end up with a graph with intersecting lines. These lines can be evenly distributed among the four quadrants or significantly clustered in one or more. There is no right or wrong distribution pattern.

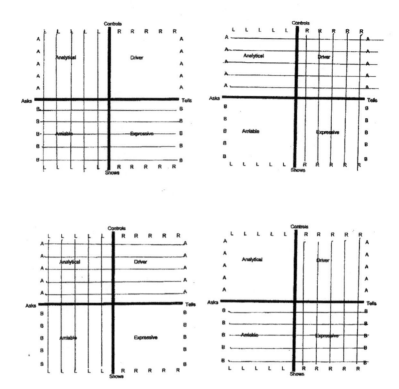

Great! What is your social style? Remember, there is no right or wrong answer here. It is what it is. You can have a combination of many styles, or just one. Remember that this test has only ten questions, and so it is not as exhaustive as some other tests. This is just a simple test to get the conversation going, and I will be speaking in general terms about social tendencies. Of course there will be exceptions to the rules. As I often heard growing up, "Eat the chicken and leave the bones." To say it another way, human behavior is very complicated and cannot always be put into one or four boxes, or even a hundred boxes.

Not everything I say here will apply to every person. These are just basic generalities about the four social styles and what your style says about how you handle anger. Your basic style will also play an important role in how you relate to others when they are angry.

So in which quadrant do most of your lines intersect? Are you a Driver, Expressive, Amiable, or Analytical? Turn to the chapter that best fits your style. You may fall into one or more category, or even a little bit of all of them. First explore the quadrant that you occupy the most, and then the others in order of their importance.

Driver: Go to chapter 19
Expressive: Go to chapter 20
Amiable: Go to chapter 21
Analytical: Go to chapter 22

The next chapter, "SOAP" discusses the relationship between your social style and clinical responses for anger. Each letter in the acronym SOAP stands for each anger style. After reading the chapter on your social style, read the next chapter to see your anger style. This is very important. Knowing your anger style will help you better understand why you do the things you do. Reading about all the social styles (reading all the chapters) will give you a greater understanding why others do what they do.

Chapter 18

SOAP

There are four basic clinical responses for anger. Each letter of the acronym SOAP stands for one of them. Each clinical response for anger corresponds with one of the four social styles:

Suppressive = Amiable
Open Aggression = Driver
Assertive = Expressive
Passive Aggression = Analytical

S Is for Suppression

We can suppress our feelings—that is, pretend they are not there. "Amiables" use the suppressive anger style. They do this so well that they may even convince themselves that they are not angry. At first, it is a conscious decision to stuff or ignore their feelings. But after a while, it becomes so natural that the suppression anger style is automatic and seems unconscious. There are many reasons for this. One reason is that Amiables are afraid of what they might do if they let their anger out. So they stuff their anger to make sure that the monster within doesn't rear its ugly head.

Another reason is that Amiables have low self-esteem. They value others as more important than themselves, and so Amiables stuff their own feelings, assuming that nobody cares about them. Besides that, Amiables do not want to rock the boat.

Sometimes we all need to make that conscious choice to suppress our anger, whether we're at work, at play, or at home, but that shouldn't be a lifestyle or a pattern. For example, when we are at work, we would be very wise to suppress or postpone our anger response, effectively asking ourselves not to think about our anger because we have a task at hand that needs our full focus. But in the end, we need to be able to share our feelings in a timely and appropriate manner in order to grow as individuals and in our relationships. It is not healthy to suppress our feelings 24/7.

O Is for Open Aggression

Open aggression, the Driver anger style, is easy to spot. Everyone knows when a Driver is angry. This open aggression can take two forms: verbal and/or physical behavior. Individuals who display their feelings in the open usually do so with little respect for others. Their goal is to communicate that they are angry—and rightfully so, from their perspective.

This open anger response fits the description of a Driver. They are goal-oriented, and when they are angry it is their goal to let you know it—plus they want to get their way, and by being intimidating and loud, they do. That is their goal. Drivers want to get their way in most situations, but this characteristic is very destructive to long-term relationships. If you are a Driver, you might find it hard to have a deep, long-term relationship with anyone. That is because people are afraid of your displays of anger and they don't want to stick around. You may win the short-term battles but lose the war.

A Is for Assertive

Assertive anger, the Expressive style, is very similar to open aggression in that everyone knows that the Expressive person is angry. The difference is how the anger is displayed. "Expressives" will show respect to the object of their anger. At the same time, they want to express their feelings, and they think everyone else should do the same. They tend to think everyone should be open to hearing and discussing feelings. But the truth is, most people think Expressives share TMI, too much information, and they find it hard to handle. Expressives are assertive with their emotions, and they like other people to share their feelings with them as well. Two Expressives may relate very well to each other. They may have emotional ups and downs, but they understand that others have the same ups and downs, and they are usually very forgiving people. Since Expressives are dreamers, they like to share and talk. Other social styles can take a cue from Expressives and learn to share their feelings while showing respect for others.

What Expressives need to learn is timing—that is, when to share—and how much to share. They need to listen and watch for other people's social clues to see if they are interested in continuing a conversation.

P Is for Passive Aggression

Individuals who are passive-aggressive in their response to anger are sneaky. This corresponds with the Analytical social style person. "Analyticals" spend time planning to get even in a way that won't get them caught. In the end, they have the satisfaction of knowing that they got their revenge. That revenge is done in secret, under the table, and behind people's backs. No one is supposed to know. So if you are an Analytical, you are an expert at being passive-aggressive in dealing with your anger. That's because you are great with details and will take the time necessary to plan getting even.

If you were to do the same thing out in the open, your response would be called open aggression. What is done in secret is passive aggression, and what is done openly is open aggression.

Passive aggression is aimed at individuals or some form of authority and is probably the most commonly used anger response in our culture. That's because there are consequences to being caught displaying anger inappropriately. So in some respects, it is wise to keep the response secret. Passive-aggressive people do not want to pay for the consequences of their response. They often feel their crime was getting caught, not committing the actual offense or payback.

Analyticals are skilled at being passive-aggressive. They have the patience and planning ability to get even at a later time and place, and if confronted about their action, they will deny any involvement in it.

One of the best examples of passive aggression is when someone asks an Analytical to do something that he/she does not want to do. He'll agree to do it, but in the end he doesn't do it. And when he is confronted, he will say, "I forgot." He really didn't want to do it, so saying he forgot is the easiest way to get away with not doing it without suffering any consequences. He knows this, and he'll plan to pretend to have forgotten when asked or confronted about it.

You can use that excuse for only so long until the other person catches on. Because if he follows up with you, you can't say you forgot over and over. It works quite well with those in authority who don't follow up, such as some parents of teenagers. Teenagers, like all of us, will say they forgot when asked to do something they don't want to do. For example, when a mom asks her teenager to clean his room, he may think, *This is my room, and I should be able to keep it the way I want it.* But if he voices his opinion to his mom, who pays the bills, it could cause World War III. Therefore, he will simply say he forgot if she confronts him about it.

Though we might use all four SOAP responses, we usually have one or two that are our basic mode of operation. Knowing yourself and your tendencies can help you change your anger response to a more appropriate one, and knowing other people's social styles can help you relate to them and understand their responses to emotional situations.

- If you have a Driver social style, then your basic anger style is Open Aggression.
- If you have an Expressive social style, then your basic anger style is Assertive.
- If you have an Amiable social style, then your basic anger style is Suppressive.
- If you have an Analytical social style, then your basic anger style is Passive Aggression.

Chapter 19

Drivers

Drivers like to be in charge. They believe they know what the best answers are for any situation. They take in the available information, come up with the best solutions to the problem, and make decisions quickly and without hesitation. They are not afraid of making mistakes. If a decision is needed, a Driver will make one.

Drivers think that if people would just listen to them and do what they say, the world would be a better place. Drivers know that they are not perfect, but they generally feel that they are right in the moment. They know that they make mistakes, but they feel that those mistakes are rare and happen under unusual circumstances. They believe that if they have control of a situation, the problems at hand can be solved. They will react swiftly to obstacles by coming up with options and suggestions and taking decisive action.

Drivers are goal-oriented. They base their decisions and actions on whatever is the best way to attain their goal(s). Drivers have the tendency to concentrate on the present while not ignoring the future or the past. They are focused on achieving their goals for today. They tend to express their opinions and conclusions decisively, directly, and confidently. Many leaders are Drivers. Their goals are to be successful, be in charge, make a difference, and be recognized, and they will work hard to achieve those goals.

On the other side of the coin, Drivers are often seen as cold, harsh, high-pressure, forceful, controlling, and independent. They can view relationships as important and necessary for reaching their goals, but not important in and of themselves. For Drivers, every relationship has its purpose in helping them achieve one of their goals. Drivers know what they want, and they want it now. They also can be nice and charming, because those qualities will help them achieve their goals.

Drivers are not necessarily mean or rude, but at their core they are not people persons, either. No doubt they can be social, charming, and the life of the party, but they are driving in a certain direction for the purpose of achieving a goal.

Chapter 20

Expressives

Expressives like to be recognized. They base their actions on dreams and intuitions. They can be dramatic, outgoing, enthusiastic, and talkative. They are very much involved in their dreams for the future and can inspire and excite those around them. They are fun to be around because they have great ideas and creativity, and they are capable of thinking outside the box. They motivate others to join them in their dreams.

On the down side, just as quickly as Expressives get excited about a dream, they can get bored with it and move on to a new, more exciting dream. They can move rapidly from one idea to another. For this reason, they appear to be imaginative and creative, but flighty. Others may view their ups and downs, their lack of staying power, as a weakness: the inability to commit to an idea and stick with it.

Expressives can make mistakes because they tend to act on hunches and intuition. Sometimes they are viewed as unorganized, unreliable, and manipulative. They are more concerned with their dreams than with reality, and so they often surround themselves with people who are good with details. Being organized is not their strength, but inspiring people and giving them a purpose to live for is their strong suit.

Chapter 21

Amiables

Amiables want to be accepted. Their priority is relationships. They are often viewed as friendly, relaxed, easygoing, and supportive. They seem to interpret the world on a totally personal level, looking for personal motivation behind every relationship.

Amiables are people persons. They often want to know who was there and what was said at work and social gatherings. They base a decision less on how it will affect them than how it will affect the other people in their lives. They don't like to rock the boat and will choose to get along with others even if it means denying their own wants and needs. They can find it hard to accept that other people can act on impersonal motivations.

Amiables tend to avoid risky or unknown situations; they like routines and sameness. They are concerned about how others feel and add personal warmth to any situation. They are great friends.

On the down side, Amiables can be viewed as weak and spineless. They are willing to go with the flow and not push their idea if it means conflicting with others. They have difficulty making decisions and choices unless they know what others want as well. Their indecisiveness may come across as not caring, but in reality they do care. They care more about people than about the activity, the way things are done, or material things.

Chapter 22

Analyticals

Analyticals are interested in the facts. Objective data, principles, and consistency are extremely important to them. While Drivers think they are right about everything, Analyticals want to be right about everything. They take time to research, consider, and ponder the available solutions before making a decision.

They are great at organizing and make good administrators, as they try to approach tasks systematically and methodically. They may seem hesitant to make a decision, but that's because they want to make sure it is the right one. This tendency can come across as a lack of enthusiasm or as indifference to others' feelings, but really it's a reflection of their concern for getting all the facts and getting it right.

Chapter 23

Session 6 Review

Session 6 is my last session of six weeks in the class I teach, and it is considered a review class. So let me take just a few moments to summarize and highlight the key points of this book.

- Anger management is essentially managing your expectations.
- Changing the way you think will change the way you feel.
- Your social style will have an impact on how you perceive and display your anger.

If your social style is

- Driver, then your basic anger style is Open Aggression.
- Expressive, then your basic anger style is Assertive.
- Amiable, then your basic anger style is Suppressive.
- Analytical, then your basic anger style is Passive Aggression,

In his book *The Power of Habit*, Charles Duhigg clearly explains that changing a habit is very possible, and that one of the keys to success is believing that the change is possible. Take time to consider the way you handle your anger, and decide to do things differently or better. You must first believe in yourself, and with that power you can begin your journey to a better you.

Thank you for spending this time with me, and I hope you live a life that exceeds your expectations.

Appendix

You use considerable body movement and/or use your hands freely	B-B OR A-A	You are controlled, stiff, and/or have limited body movement
You tends to lean back, not face to face in communication, occasional eye contact	L-L OR R-R	You tends to lean forward, faces others squarely-holds constant eye contact
You are cool, distant, guarded in relationships	A-A OR B-B	You are warm, friendly, and emotional in relationships
You are quick, fast pace, strong, and/or demanding speech	R-R OR L-L	You are deliberate, slow pace, quiet, and/or unassuming speech
You have unresponsive facial expressions, more of a "poker face"	A-A OR B-B	You have responsive, animated facial expressions, smiles and frowns a lot
Your communication is to the point, clear, definitive	R-R OR L-L	Your communication is vague and indefinite, like to tell a story
Your viewpoints are open, expresses opinions, little emphasis on specific details	B-B OR A-A	Your viewpoints are cautious, careful, with emphasis upon facts and specific details
You use moderate use of voice, make limited effort to take a stand, leaves situations unresolved	L-L OR R-R	You use moderate voice to emphasize points, takes a stand, presses for a decision
You are generally serious, thoughtful, and/or critical	A-A OR B-B	You are mostly playful, fun-loving, joking around
Your facial expressions suggests supportive, cooperative attitudes	L-L OR R-R	Your facial expressions suggest dominant, competitive attitudes

Circle the two letters on the best side of the middle column that best reflects you. For example: if you choose the left column on the first column, then circle the letters B-B. If you choose the right side, then circle A-A. Choose and circle the rest of the letters that best reflect you. There is no right or wrong answers. Try not to get stuck, pick the one the best represents the way you relate to others.

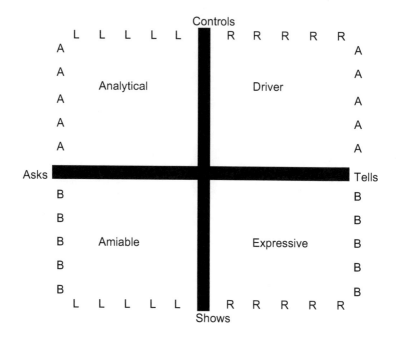

From your answers from the previous page connect the two letters starting from the center of the graph, then work your way towards the edge of the graph top, bottom, left or right edges. See sample below for getting started. You should have graph with intersecting lines. These lines can be evenly distributed in each quadrant or significantly in one or the other. There is not right or wrong graph.

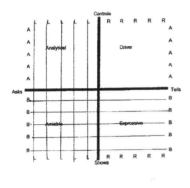

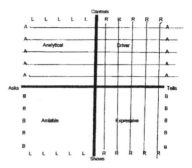

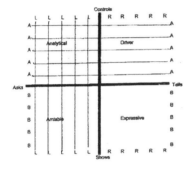

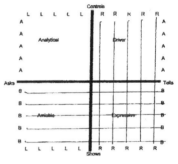

Bibliography

Benner, D. *Bake Encyclopedia of Psychology*. Grand Rapids, MI: Baker Book House, 1985.

Burns, David. *Feeling Good*. Avon.

Collins, Gary. *Self-Talk, Imagery and Prayer in Counseling*. Dallas: Word Publishing, 1986.

Feist, J. *Theories of Personality*. Chicago: Holt, Rinehart and Winston, 1990.

Hafner, Jack. *Anger: Discover Your Personal Power to Change*. Center City, MN: Hazelden Foundation Materials.

McKay, M. *Thoughts and Feelings*. Oakland, CA: New Harbinger Publications, 1981.

Meyer, Minith. *The Complete Life Encyclopedia*. Nashville: Thomas Nelson, 1995.

Systema Corp. *The Sales Relationship*. Chicago: Systema.

Travis, Carol. *Anger, the Misunderstood Emotion*. New York: Simon and Schuster.

Author's note: I must also give credit to the many articles I read, seminars I attended, and conversations I had with professionals during my life journey.

Edwards Brothers Malloy
Thorofare, NJ USA
September 1, 2016